1979

ASPECTS OF EVE

Also by *Linda Pastan*

A PERFECT CIRCLE OF SUN
ON THE WAY TO THE ZOO

ASPECTS OF EVE

POEMS BY
Linda Pastan

LIVERIGHT  NEW YORK

Acknowledgment is gratefully made to the following magazines in which these poems appeared: *American Poetry Review*, which published "Knots," "Short Story"; *The American Scholar*, which published "A Sense of Direction"; *Audience*, which published "To a Daughter"; *Chelsea*, which published "Folk Tale" *Choice*, which published "Go Gentle"; *The Chowder Review*, which published "Sacred to Apollo"; *Dryad*, which published "Cape Cod–Israel," "Letter," "On Watching the Israeli War on TV"; *Esquire*, which published "Swimming Last Summer," "Hurricane Watch"; *Field*, which published "To Consider a House," "Eclipse," "Death's Blue-eyed Girl"; *Hanging Loose*, which published "Soul Song"; *Harper's*, which published "After Agatha Christie"; *The Hawaii Review*, which published "Clytemnestra," "You Are Odysseus"; *Koutomie*, which published "Night"; *Lillabulero*, which published "Night Sounds"; *Mill Mountain Review*, which published "Popcorn"; *Ms*, which published "At the Armed Borders of Sleep"; *The New York Times*, which published "On Going to Sweden for My Fortieth Birthday," "The Ides of March," "Algebra"; *Perspective*, which published "Aspects of Eve"; *Poetry for Public Places*, which published "To a Daughter"; *Poetry Now*, which published "Grief," "Rachel"; *Radcliffe Quarterly*, which published "Pass/Fail"; *Response*, which published "David"; *South Carolina Review*, which published "Block"; *Southern Poetry Review*, which published "Drift"; *Southern Voices*, which published "Butter."

Cold Mountain Press published "A Real Story" in broadsheet form.

The following poems appeared in the chapbook *On the Way to the Zoo*, published by *Dryad*: "Folk Tale," "Night Sounds," "Soul Song."

I would like to thank the National Endowment for Arts and Humanities for a grant which helped me write some of these poems.

Three lines from "Eve's Exile" by Archibald MacLeish are reprinted here by kind permission of the publisher, Houghton Mifflin, from the volume *Songs for Eve* by Archibald MacLeish.

FIRST EDITION

Library of Congress Cataloging in Publication Data
Pastan, Linda, 1932–
    Aspects of Eve.

    I. Title.
PS3566.A775A93   811'.5'4   75-6557
ISBN 0-87140-608-X
ISBN 0-87140-102-9 pbk.

Published simultaneously in Canada
by George J. McLeod Limited, Toronto
PRINTED IN THE UNITED STATES OF AMERICA

1 2 3 4 5 6 7 8 9 0

For *Stephen, Peter,* and *Rachel*

Space within its time revolves
But Eve must spin as Adam delves
Because our exile is ourselves.

Archibald MacLeish: "Eve's Exile"

Contents

Because Our Exile Is Ourselves

Space within Its
Time Revolves

RACHEL

(Rachel [rā'chal], a ewe)

We named you
for the sake
of the syllables
and for the small boat
that followed the *Pequod*,
gathering lost children
of the sea.

We named you
for the dark-eyed girl
who waited at the well
while her lover
worked seven years
and again
seven.

We named you
for the small daughters
of the Holocaust
who followed their six-pointed stars
to death
and were all of them
known as
Rachel.

NIGHT SOUNDS

When the clock
like a moon shows
the dark side of its face
we reach
across cold expanses
of pillow
for speech.
In that silence
a fox barks
from the next field,
or a train drags its long syllable
over a hill,
or the baby
washed up again from sleep
sends its vowels
calling
for their lost
consonants.

A REAL STORY

Sucking on hard candy
to sweeten the taste
of old age,
grandpa told us stories
about chickens,
city chickens sold
for Sabbath soup
but rescued at the end
by some chicken-loving
providence.

Now at ninety-five,
sucked down
to nothing himself,
he says he feels
a coldness;
perhaps the coldness David felt
even with Abishag
in his bed
to warm
his chicken-thin bones.

But when we say
you'll soon get well,
grandpa pulls the sheet
over his face,
raising it between us
the way he used to raise
the Yiddish paper
when we said
enough chickens
tell us a real story.

GO GENTLE

You have grown wings of pain
and flap around the bed like a wounded gull
calling for water, calling for tea, for grapes
whose skins you cannot penetrate.
Remember when you taught me
how to swim? Let go, you said,
the lake will hold you up.
I long to say, Father let go
and death will hold you up.
Outside the fall goes on without us.
How easily the leaves give in,
I hear them on the last breath of wind,
passing this disappearing place.

THE PRUNING

The aerialist of the woods
on his trapeze
prunes my oak trees
cuts off the scarred knuckles
and the bruised limbs
painting the wounded bark
where woodpeckers
on other mornings
drill bugs to their
small deaths.

Nearby his partner
with a yellow chain saw
buzzes
like a monster bee
gone mad,
cuts into neat stacks
for firewood
crutches and braces
splints and trusses:
all this deadened wood.

I think of you,
old friend
pruned back by surgeons
to the gnarled bone,
waiting
for some new leafing
some green,
unlikely
spring.

WILDFLOWERS

You gave me dandelions.
They took our lawn
by squatters' rights—
round suns rising
in April, soft moons
blowing away in June.
You gave me lady slippers,
bloodroot, milkweed,
trillium whose secret number
the children you gave me
tell. In the hierarchy
of flowers, the wild
rise on their stems
for naming.
Call them weeds.
I pick them as I
picked you,
for their fierce,
unruly joy.

TO A DAUGHTER

Knit two, purl two.
I make of small boredoms
a fabric
to keep you warm.
Is it my own image
I love so
in your face?
I lean over your sleep,
Narcissus over
his clear pool,
ready to fall in—
to drown for you,
if necessary.

ON GOING TO SWEDEN FOR
MY FORTIETH BIRTHDAY

On the evening
of another departure,
I am framed by this window
as if I were a portrait
that has always hung
in this house.
My place is here safe
among the smooth linens
folded away on shelves—
I would be folded so;
or tucked into a drawer of spoons
as the children are tucked,
knees drawn up,
in their small beds upstairs.
Here as in Sweden
it is early spring,
but this landscape unfurls
so swiftly into summer:
the fuzzy adolescent grass
deepens, even as I stand,
to its full resonance of green.
All that is started here
will be ending,
middle age will welcome me back,
even the dogwood
which tells so shyly
its new vocation of white
will be rosy, matronly
with berries
by then.

FOLK TALE

I

All knobs and knuckles, hammer knees and elbows
they were a multitude of two, man and woman
dwelling as one tight flesh. In hallways,
on stairs vaguely lit by twilight, in their own
meager bed they would collide . . . veer off . . .
collide, like aging children aiming those
bumper cars, madly in Kansas Coney Islands.
Blue sparks jumped on their ceiling, lit her stockings
strangling his faucet, his fist plumbing
her shoulder's depth for blood. Until, as it is told,
they brought the cow into the house, straight from the barn,
oppressed for years with milk. They tied it,
lowing, to the icebox, pastured it
on rubber plants and dusty philodendrons.
They brought the horse in next, leaving the plow
like an abandoned aircraft, nose down
in rusting fields of corn. The pig, the donkey,
the rooster with its crowd of hens, they even
brought a neighbor's child complete with spelling words
and scales that wandered up and down the untuned
piano searching for roost as the chickens
searched and the cow, nuzzling the humming
frigidaire as if it were a calf.

II

So they survived with all that cuckoo's brood,
hearing the horse stamp through the floorboards,
the donkey chew the welcome mat, and all night long
through tumbling barricades of sleep the yeasty
rise and fall of breath. By blue television light
they milked and gathered, boiled the placid eggs
that turned up everywhere, laughed with the child,

fed the pig, and glimpsed each other's rounded limbs
reflected for a moment in the copper
washtub or around the feathers of a settling hen.
And winter passed; and spring; and summer.
The child left first, all braided, for the school bus.
The cow died of old griefs. The horse dreaming
of harness, the pig of swill, the donkey
of what magnitude of straw, broke out one night
and emptied the ark. Man and woman leaning
on brooms stood at the kitchen door and waved,
saw through a blaze of autumn the cock's comb
like one last, bright leaf flutter and disappear.
Then jostling a bit, for ceremony's sake,
they turned and lost themselves in so much space.

DEATH'S BLUE-EYED GIRL

When did the garden with its banked flowers
start to smell like a funeral chapel,
and the mild breeze passing our foreheads
to feel like the back of a nurse's hand
testing for fever? We used to be
immortal in our ignorance, sending
our kites up for the lightning, swimming
in unknown waters at night and naked.
Death was a kind of safety net to catch us
if we fell too far. Remember Elaine
standing in April, a child on one hip
for ballast, her head distracted with poems?
The magician waved and bowed, showed us his
empty sleeves and she was gone.

SHORT STORY

In the short story
that is my life
the mother and the father
who were there from the beginning
have started to disappear.
Now the lover repeats
his one line, and the plot
instead of thickening
as it might, thins
almost to blank paper.
There is no epiphany.
Even an animal whose cry
seemed symbolic
has lapped its milk
and gone quietly
to sleep. And though
there is room for a brief
descriptive passage (perhaps
a snowfall, some
stiffening of the weather)
already
it is dark
on the other side
of the page.

GRIEF

How did your grief
enter my poem?
Now it is an unwieldy package
between us—
you balanced it better alone.
Your son's cells
close down
one by one,
like lights going out
in a small town
after dark.
Writing of it
I must wash and wash my hands
of the ink.

TO CONSIDER A HOUSE

"Eden is that old fashioned house we dwell in every
day . . ."

Emily Dickinson

When Eden closed like a fist
around a penny,
like a flower whose petals contract
at the first touch
of weather,
when only fire was left to warn,
as fire warns the wild animal;
and even before Cain
had come to start
what we have never ended;
it was time then, for the first time,
to consider a house.
Before, they had rested
carelessly, naming a tree
then sleeping under it,
or sleeping first
and naming later. Now,
the soul shaken loose
from the body,
in temporary residence only
in their skin,
they dreamed the safety
of boxes within boxes,
of doors closing quietly
on doors.
They traveled East,
not following the sun
but drawn, as if by accident, back
to its source.

The animals too had fled, taking
only their names with them.
So as the birds learned,
they learned
to build of scraps,
of sticks and straws collected
along the way.
With the beaver they saw
what can be dammed up,
how to make use of all
that accumulates.
And like the bear they took
the hollowness of caves,
a shape to be confirmed
by the still untested womb.
In their own image they build their house:
eyelike windows, blank
with light; a skeleton of beams;
clay walls, crumbling a little,
as flesh was already learning
to crumble.
And from the hearth,
the smoldering center of the house, smoke
rose up the chimney
each morning, each dusk
making the leap toward God
that always ended
in cloud.
Only much later,
and hesitantly at first,
they thought to plant
another garden.

But Eve Must Spin
as Adam Delves

YOU ARE ODYSSEUS

You are Odysseus
returning home each evening
tentative, a little angry.
And I who thought to be
one of the Sirens (cast up
on strewn sheets
at dawn)
hide my song
under my tongue—
merely Penelope after all.
Meanwhile the old wars
go on, their dim music
can be heard even at night.
You leave each morning,
soon our son will follow.
Only my weaving is real.

BUTTER

You held the butter-
cup under my chin
and laughed: "get thee
to a buttery,"
chewing on a dandelion stem,
then tasting my
buttery fingers
one by one
and eying
my breasts as if
they too could,
bobbing, churn
pure milk to
butter.
Yellow dress and
flowers, yellow
hair, the world
was melting butter
sweet and slick,
your hands all yellow
with the spilling
sun, desire
like the heated
knife through
butter.

KNOTS

In the retreating tide
of light,
among bulrushes
and eel grass
my small son teaches
my stuttering hands
the language of sailor's knots.

I tell him how
each Jewish bride
was given a knotted chaos
of yarn
and told to order it
into a perfect sphere,
to prove she'd be a patient wife.

Patient, impatient son
I've unknotted shoestrings,
kitestrings, tangled hair.
But standing at high windows
enclosed in the domestic rustle
of birds and leaves
I've dreamed of knotting
bedsheets together
to flee by.

SWIMMING LAST SUMMER

Swimming last summer in sun-kindled water,
hand in hand,
we had to surface dive to find
those cold currents
that run like harp chords counterpoint
to the lake's heat.

Still touching,
we swam between them, from cold
to cold, like children
in a field of scattered trees
running from shade to shade
for rest.

Now, in January,
the cold has risen to the top like cream,
curdling through the grassy shallows,
sharp as mica by the shore,
and at the lake's dead center
thick, opaque, reflecting neither casual cloud
nor shadows of a passing gull's wing.

Just so your eyes,
rippling toward my shore all summer
now become glazed and cold,
your thoughts of me more sluggish than
some winter-dazed trout
swimming as close to bottom as it dares.

And maddened,
I long to beat your head with my fists
to chop through the freezing crust like an Eskimo
and fish you back
with nothing but string and a hook
and my remembered body
for bait.

CAPE COD-ISRAEL

(for Amichai)

I am reading your poems
here by the edge of my sea.
Nearby, children in orange life vests
scrabble like lobsters over the sand,
and the cultures of mackerel
and crab merge
in the common language of water.

By your sea
do you read my poems, near Galilee
where the crossed masts of ships
still wait for their one prophet,
and the surf unrolls its heavy
scroll of salt?

If we swim
toward each other, you and I,
each from his own shore,
though the waves go down
on their knees in the sand
how soon will we sink?

BLOCK

I place one word slowly
in front of the other,
like learning to walk again
after an illness.
But the blank page
with its hospital corners
tempts me.
I want to lie down
in its whiteness
and let myself drift
all the way back
to silence.

DRIFT

Lying in bed this morning
you read to me of continental drift,
how Africa and South America
sleeping once side by side
slowly slid apart;
how California even now
pushes off like a swimmer
from the country's edge, along
the San Andreas fault.
And I thought about you and me
who move in sleep each night
to the far reaches of the bed,
ranges of blanket between us.
It is a natural law this drift
and though we break it
as we break bread
over and over again, you remain
Africa with your deep shade,
your heat. And I, like California,
push off from your side
my two feet cold
against your back, dreaming
of Asia Minor.

PASS/FAIL

"Examination dreams are reported to persist even
into old age . . ."

Time magazine

You will never graduate
from this dream
of blue books.
No matter how
you succeed awake,
asleep there is a test
waiting to be failed.
The dream beckons
with two dull pencils,
but you haven't even
taken the course;
when you reach for a book—
it closes its door
in your face; when
you conjugate a verb—
it is in the wrong
language.
Now the pillow becomes
a blank page. Turn it
to the cool side;
you will still smother
in all of the feathers
that have to be learned
by heart.

POETRY READING

I am the bride
waiting in the hall
for guests to gather.
No one comes.
I shall read
to the chairs—
used to the poetry
of bodies
they will remain
straight-backed,
hardly creaking;
now come the aunts,
the cousins.
I am the baby
intoning my name
at my own christening,
anointing my bare skull
with words.
I read a poem,
another.
The faces watch,
the smiles are wrapped
in pink bows,
like shower gifts.
I am the bar mitzvah boy,
each poem is a ceremony
I must perform.
Words leap
from my tongue
like mice from the mouths
of bishops
in the painting by Bosch.
And the heads
so solemn
nod iambically.
They are rehearsing
for my funeral.

LETTER

I am blinded by the glare
of blank paper.
Words hover like flies—
buzz around my head,
but will not settle.
What can I say
that blank paper cannot say
more gently?
Even the weather
is a dangerous subject
between us.
It is raining.
We met in rain and might as well
have stayed, each isolated
by his own umbrella.
I trust you're well,
that reading this you'll note,
in the downward slope
of my sentences,
a nature always asking
for the worst;
that in my tight *rs*,
my closed *es*, you'll recognize
everything that has happened
between us—enough.
I am darkening the page.
I have bitten another pencil
to the quick.

SOUNDINGS

"And deeper than did ever plummet sound/I'll
drown my book."
Shakespeare: The Tempest

If you drop a closed book
into a pail of water,
will it open like one of those
Chinese water flowers,
and bloom?
Will the characters
who were simply jogging along
leap
from its pages and swim
out of the pail?
All these years the books
have stood mute
on their shelves,
spine to spine,
Lilar up against Lilith,
Odysseus landlocked
at last
between the *Iliad*
and Orwell.
I have walked through this room
eating an apple, thinking
idly about suicide. Now
like some casual God I point my finger
at one book, open it—
it jerks to life crying, shouting,
making jokes at my expense,
talking, talking.
(It is the aviary at night:
the birds sleep perched

upon shelves, and I come,
throwing off covers
lighting lights, until
they open wings like moulting fans
and sing and fly
away.)
I pace this room of shelves
where books sit in their open graves
upright,
like the early Japanese dead,
reducing the world to words,
the words to letters,
the letters to intricate traps
that trip me until I fall,
dragging a bookcase with me.
And I drown
in the loosed wave of language.

CLYTEMNESTRA

We punish ourselves
with children.
They run through our heads
all day
Like small, harsh tunes.
Like words they have escaped
onto the page
where we cannot change them.
The babies have died,
they are dead I say.
The children they've left
in their place
stare out of our eyes
into our faces, then
wave us away,
if they remember to wave
at all.

SACRED TO APOLLO

Sometimes I am Daphne.
My sleeves rustle
in the wind,
and I feel the green root
of the bay, nourishing
or aching with the season.

And I have been Niobe,
all mother,
all tears,
but myself
somewhere hidden
in the essential stone.

You say I write
like a man
and expect me
to smile.

Or you hold me as though
I would break;
and indeed I come apart
in your hands
like pieces of a vast
and unsolved puzzle.

Perhaps it is Apollo
I still flee from,
despite his music
and his healing ways.

Now I paint my mouth
red for blood,
and in its twistings,
secret as any river,
I am Helen again
and dangerous.

A SENSE OF DIRECTION

On my north side only moss grows,
in the steep shade of the mind
where tendrils of rose cling
but are cut back at the root.
To the south colors burst
and fade with the season,
fickle as grass you cover me
but are soon gone.
I have even pursued the sun
east to west,
have seen its last awful fall
over the edge
and followed instead a cold compass home,
to the still, green certainty of moss.

ARTIFICER

Blindfold
I follow the thread
of a poem
wherever it leads,
remembering the labyrinth,
remembering Daedalus
for whom I named
my first son:
Stephen.
I follow the thread
inward,
through hives of cells
each storing its one
perfect image.
They call the self
a dark wood.
When I uncover
my face
I am in a clearing
painfully small,
surrounded
by the barbed wire
of my own
alphabet.

ASPECTS OF EVE

To have been one
of many ribs
and to be chosen.
To grow into something
quite different
knocking finally
as a bone knocks
on the closed gates of the garden—
which unexpectedly
open.

Because Our Exile
Is Ourselves

HURRICANE WATCH

I saw once,
through the eyepiece of a microscope,
a blizzard of cells.
And at times
the hairs on my arm lift,
as if in some incalculable wind,
or my throat echoes
the first hoarse forecast
of thunder.
Some live in the storm's eye only.
I rise and fall
with the barometer,
holding on for my life.
Here, in a storm cellar
of flesh,
pale as the roots I live on,
I read my palm
as though it were a weather map
and keep a hurricane watch
all year.

THE IDES OF MARCH

The spring holds off . . .
holds off. Trees
have forgotten their leaves already.
Like a snake chilled
by the stone it sleeps on,
I seek some warm-blooded body
to lean against.
After years, I dreamed of
you again. This morning
I know it is possible
to drown in a dead sea.

Birds have eaten my path
of crumbs.
Who can promise that even spring
will blunder through the woods
home?

AFTER AGATHA CHRISTIE

in the locked room
what cannot happen
happens again
shaped to the size
of a keyhole
death comes reassuring
choosing someone
no one will miss
now everything becomes
a clue
the moon has left
footprints
all over the rug
the tree outside
the window
hides behind
its false beard
of leaves
who did what
precisely when
slyly the clock stops
the blood smells of ink
the revolver shows
its pearl handle
at the end the facts
click into place
comfortably as knitting
each answer marries
its proper question
even the skull
smiles to itself
as the detective tells
how the moon was pure
all along
the tree was merely
a tree
and only I
have no alibi
at all

AN EVENING OUT

I have wandered into Chekhov
by pure accident,
mistaking the strokes
of my own heart
for the sound of an ax
against a tree
far away in the orchard.
But they have let me in.
The old family retainer
serves me, saying:
before the calamity
the same thing happened,
the owl screeched and the samovar
hummed all the time.
I hear no owl.
But drinking coffee, I dream
calamities of my own—
evenings like this, for instance,
my life which has gone by
as though I'd never lived.
I speak at random of the season
to a man in a gray vest
who mentions the weather.
But though he is polite,
it is clearly the dark-eyed girl
he admires most, and indeed
she is more slender than I.
Meanwhile, nothing much occurs.
We are waiting for something,
a shot, perhaps,
but here only a car misfires somewhere
in the empty street, and night
comes down over the sky
like the fourth act curtain
velvety and dark
finally falling.

POPCORN

When Plato said
that what we see are shadows
flickering on a cave wall,
he must have meant
the movies.
You let a cigarette lean
from your mouth precisely
as Bogart did.
Because of this, reels later,
we say of our life
that it is B-grade;
that it opened and will close
in a dusty place where
things move always
in slow motion;
that what is real
is the popcorn
jammed between our teeth.

NIGHT

I slip
out of my skin
each night,
hold it up by the sleeves
to see its shape,
examining the fabric,
noticing
how it has started
to give
at the finely sewn
seams. Then
I slip gently
back into it
to sleep.

But night presses
against the window.
This bed can only carry me
on the same journey
from which I keep returning
a little older.
And in dreams
where what has been lost
is sometimes so briefly
found, I slip
out of my skin again
half hoping
not to find my way
back in.

MINI BLUES

Like a dinghy
I always lag
behind, awash
in somebody else's wake.
Or I answer
the low call
of the foghorn,
only to find
that what it meant
was keep away.

SOUL SONG

The snake slips from its skins,
leaving ghosts of itself
to haunt rocks
and the furrows
of fields. Still it remains
solid and supple as ever,
no closer to the marrow
of snake.

And the onion whose simple secret
I think to uncover layer
by transparent layer
leaves nothing, finally,
for the hand to close on
but pungency.

Yet there is something
hard as a peach pit to which
the flesh clings stubbornly.
I feel it move in the lonely cavity
of the chest, or high up in the skull
like a queen bee that must
be evicted in the end
from the hive.

ON WATCHING THE
ISRAELI WAR ON TV

We are Jews after all
though Narragansett summers
have salted our bones dry
and blown out our candles
in a wind from the midwest.
What is this old anger
unreasoned as tears?
We grow our alien corn
from chosen seed
bought in packets
at the corner hardware store.
We thresh it, grind it,
send Care packages of it
in our own unexplained absence.

AT THE ARMED
BORDERS OF SLEEP

touch me
says Harold
this is only a dream
so be quick
about it

It is a March day,
full of shadow.
Like an underground river a dream
surfaces
and is gone again
in shadow.

I move through cities
of sleep, past buildings
I lived in, or
thought to live in, and on
into the heart's suburb.
Here fear becomes simple.
Even the animals seem familiar,
they eat from my hand
while the roots of trees
tangle darkly with the roots
of my hair. But listen:
the wind is as violent as breath.
The hum of bees is the hum
of blood, swarming
out of a hive
of cells.

ah, be quick
about it.

There is light
assembling.
Perhaps it is morning
or the mother of morning.
I turn my back
on it.

At the armed borders of sleep
my dreams stand waving.
I brush my teeth,
eat breakfast,
dress.
The sun moves from darkness
to darkness, picking
its way
through the day's foliage.
I work at my desk,
drink tea.
They are still
waving.

DAVID

this one, said the sculptor, is the last of the biblical figures

The last of the biblical figures
is David, carved
from the trunk of an ash.
If we place him in our rooms
he will make music.
If we burn him in our stoves
he will give heat.
The ash comes to flower
again, each leaf
is a note the harp plays.
And as the sap rises
the word lifts
to the mouth to be spoken.
David.
The knots of your tree
break the teeth of our saws.
The book will outlast
even its pages.

ALGEBRA

I used to solve equations easily.
If train A left Sioux Falls
at nine o'clock, traveling
at a fixed rate,
I knew when it would meet train B.
Now I wonder if the trains will crash;
or else I picture naked limbs
through Pullman windows, each
a small vignette of longing.

And I knew X, or thought I did,
shuttled it back and forth
like a poor goat
across the equals sign.
X was the unknown on a motor bike,
those autumn days when leaves flew past
the color of pencil shavings.
Obedient as a genie, it gave me answers
to what I thought were questions.

Unsolved equations later, and winter now,
I know X better than I did.
His is the scarecrow's bitter mouth
sewn shut in cross-stitch;
the footprint of a weasel on snow.
X is the unknown assailant.
X marks the spot
toward which we speed like trains,
at a fixed rate.

ECLIPSE

A few minutes past noon:
the birds begin their evening songs
and break for the trees;
the horse nods in its dimming stall.
Afraid of a truth that could blind
I turn my cold shoulder to the sun
and catch its shadow in a cardboard box
as though it were some rare bug
about to be effaced by the moon's
slow thumb. To catalog is not enough.
What did Adam know, naming the apple?
What do the astronomers suspect?
The sun like a swallowed sword
comes blazing back.
It is not chaos
I fear in this strange dusk
but the inexplicable order of things.

A SYMPOSIUM: APPLES

Eve: Remember a season
of apples, the orchard
full of them, my apron
full of them. One day
we wandered from tree
to tree, sharing a basket
feeling the weight of apples
increase between us.
And how your muscles ripened
with all that lifting.
I felt them round and hard
under my teeth; white
and sweet the flesh
of men and apples.

Gabriel: Nameless in Eden,
the apple itself
was innocent—an ordinary
lunchpail fruit.
Still it reddened
for the way it was used.
Afterward the apple
chose for itself
names untrusting
on the tongue: stayman,
gravenstein,
northern spy.

The Serpent: Ordinary, innocent
yes. But deep
in each center of whiteness
one dark star . . .

Adam: In the icebox
an apple

will keep
for weeks.
Then its skin
wrinkles up
like the skin of the old man
I have become,
from a single
bite.